THE CARS & TRUCKS COLORING BOOK

By Jerry Gonzalez

ISBN-13: 978-0998247304 (JG Graphics LLC)
ISBN-10: 0998247308

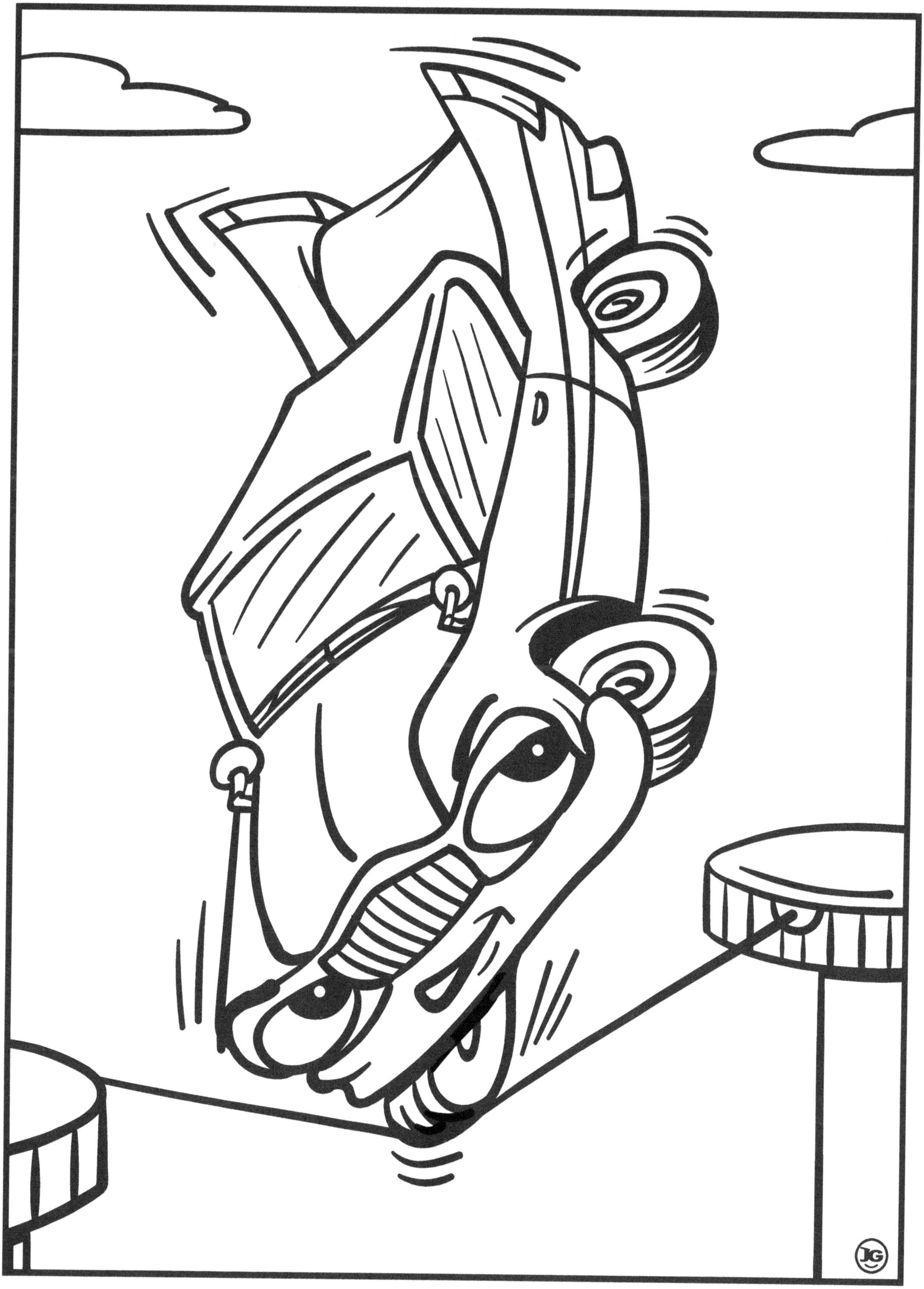

www.ingramcontent.com/pod-product-compliance
Lightning Source LLC
Chambersburg PA
CBHW081303040426
42452CB00014B/2634
9780998247304